OMG WTF IS GERRYMANDERING?

OMG WTF IS GERRYMANDERING?

A JOURNAL FOR
CONCERNED CITIZENS

BEN SHEEHAN
AND ARIELLE YUSPEH

BLACK DOG
& LEVENTHAL
PUBLISHERS
NEW YORK

Black Dog & Leventhal Publishers
Hachette Book Group
1290 Avenue of the Americas
New York, NY 10104

www.hachettebookgroup.com
www.blackdogandleventhal.com

First Edition: April 2020

Black Dog & Leventhal Publishers is an imprint of Perseus Books, LLC,
a subsidiary of Hachette Book Group, Inc. The Black Dog & Leventhal
Publishers name and logo are trademarks of Hachette Book Group, Inc.

The publisher is not responsible for websites (or their content)
that are not owned by the publisher.

The Hachette Speakers Bureau provides a wide range of authors for speaking events.
To find out more, go to www.HachetteSpeakersBureau.com or call (866) 376-6591.

Print book interior design by Katie Benezra

LCCN: 2019948147
ISBN: 978-0-7624-9845-1

Printed in Singapore

1010

10 9 8 7 6 5 4 3 2 1

WHAT IS "GERRYMANDERING"?

SHORT ANSWER:

A dumb word for drawing districts that favor a group of people, with the goal of winning certain elections. It isn't always illegal, but it IS always cheating.

LONG(ER) ANSWER:

A district is an area of land, and the residents of that area are the district's "constituents." Constituents elect their district's representatives, and these representatives are meant to look out for those constituents' interests. Examples of governing bodies with districts include the US House of Representatives (federal legislature), state houses and state senates (state legislatures), and city councils and school boards (local legislatures).

Every 10 years, the US Constitution requires us to "enumerate" (determine the number of) representatives in the US House of Representatives from each state, based on its population. As populations in different places change, districts should be redrawn to ensure that they each have an equal number of people in them (regardless of land size). We do this with the census by counting the whole population, and then each state, county, and city redraws its districts from the data (which includes things like your name, sex, age, race, and ethnicity). This is called "redistricting."

However, each state has its own process for drawing districts for US House and state legislative seats (as does each county and city). Sometimes districts are drawn by an independent commission of nonpoliticians (ordinary citizens); ideally, these commissions consist of an equal number of Democrats and Republicans...

Some states have a political committee, where an equal number of elected or appointed politicians from each party draws the districts...

But in *most* states, the state legislature draws the US House, state house, and state senate district lines. So in theory, if the state legislature was controlled by one party, they could exploit the census data to draw all of the districts in a way that favors their party. And lastly, it's not a theory...states do this *all the fucking time*. This is "partisan gerrymandering."

But how do state legislatures draw districts to favor one party? By utilizing that census data to "pack" and "crack" certain voters into specific districts. These state legislators can draw districts so that the other party's voters are concentrated in only a few districts. That way, they'll have less of an impact on the rest of the state. That's "packing." Or legislators can break them up, or "crack" them, so that members of the other party are spread across many districts, where they'll be less likely to have an impact in *any* district.

Today it's illegal to gerrymander based on the race, sex, or preferred language of voters. But it *isn't* illegal to gerrymander based on their political party. So until Congress passes a law that bans partisan gerrymandering, or each state makes it illegal by creating a fair redistricting process, gerrymandering will continue.

But you can help. You can push your state legislators (your state representative and your state senator) to establish an independent redistricting commission if it doesn't already exist in your state. You can pressure your federal legislators (your US Representative and your US Senators) to introduce, or support, a bill that establishes independent commissions in *every* state. Or you could support a ballot measure or a constitutional amendment (if your state allows) that establishes an independent redistricting commission. Or, if there isn't one in motion, start your own. Katie Fahey did just that, and in 2018 she helped end gerrymandering in Michigan.

Perhaps you can fight gerrymandering by writing your plans to end it in this gerrymander-themed journal. Or just use it for grocery lists. Honestly, no pressure.

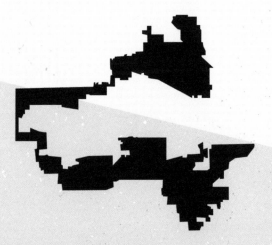

ILLINOIS
US Congressional District 4

_____

_____

_____

_____

_____

_____

_____

_____

_____

_____

_____

_____

_____

_____

_____

_____

In 1812, then Massachusetts Governor Elbridge Gerry approved new state senate districts that were drawn by the state legislature. These new district lines were hugely manipulated in order to favor his Democratic-Republican party (a real party at the time). In fact, one of the districts was so distorted that it resembled a salamander. This new district map—adorned with added claws, wings, and fangs—was published in the Boston *Weekly Messenger* under the title *The Gerry-Mander*. That is the origin of this very dumb term.

Texas's 35th Congressional District goes to great lengths—literally 80 miles—to pack Austin's black voters and San Antonio's Hispanic voters into the same long, thin district. Despite multiple federal district court rulings that the Texas legislature intentionally drew the district "based on race," and that it was "an impermissible racial gerrymander," in 2018 the US Supreme Court ruled that the district was allowed to stand.

AUSTIN →

SAN ANTONIO →

TEXAS

US Congressional District 35

That's all we're asking for: an end to the antidemocratic and un-American practice of gerrymandering congressional districts.

−PRESIDENT RONALD REAGAN, MARCH 22, 1988

There are two main ways to gerrymander—**"packing"** and **"cracking."**

Ohio's 1st Congressional District "**cracks**" just the right amount of Democrats in Cincinnati's Hamilton County, so that they'll always be slightly overpowered by the Republican-dominated Warren County.

← CINCINNATI

OHIO

US Congressional District 1

_____

_____

_____

_____

_____

_____

_____

_____

_____

_____

_____

_____

_____

_____

_____

_____

_____

_____

_____

_____

_____

We've got to end the practice of drawing our congressional districts
so that politicians can pick their voters, and not the other way around.
Let a bipartisan group do it.

–PRESIDENT BARACK OBAMA, JANUARY 12, 2016

Throughout the 1980s, California was badly gerrymandered to favor Democrats across its US House, state assembly (house), and state senate districts. Today, because of the tireless efforts of individuals such as former governor Arnold Schwarzenegger, California has an independent redistricting commission that draws its lines fairly, so that Republican voters are not disenfranchised.

Gerrymandering occurs across all levels of government—US House of Representatives, state legislatures, and even city councils and school boards.

"**Hijacking**" redraws two districts in such a way as to force two incumbents to run against each other in one district, ensuring that one of them will be eliminated.

Louisiana's 6th Congressional District, which encompasses most of Baton Rouge, is missing its African-American neighborhoods. You'll find them in Louisiana's neighboring 2nd Congressional District, having been cut out of Louisiana's 6th Congressional District to keep the state capital reliably Republican.

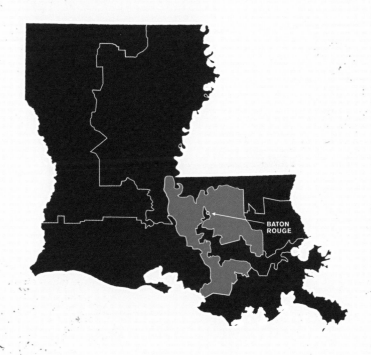

BATON
ROUGE

LOUISIANA

US Congressional District 6

_____

_____

_____

_____

_____

_____

_____

_____

_____

_____

_____

_____

_____

_____

_____

_____

_____

_____

_____

_____

_____

_____

Gerrymandering has completely broken our political system.

**–FORMER CALIFORNIA GOVERNOR
ARNOLD SCHWARZENEGGER, MARCH 12, 2017**

_____

_____

_____

_____

_____

_____

_____

_____

_____

_____

_____

_____

_____

_____

_____

_____

_____

Although the Voting Rights Act of 1965 outlaws gerrymandering along racial or language lines, **there is no federal law that makes it illegal to gerrymander along political party lines.**

Here is a thought:
We should have that law.

_____

_____

_____

_____

_____

_____

_____

_____

_____

_____

_____

_____

_____

_____

_____

_____

_____

_____

_____

_____

_____

_____

_____

_____

"Kidnapping" moves an incumbent's home address into another district.

_____

_____

_____

_____

_____

_____

_____

_____

_____

_____

_____

_____

_____

_____

_____

_____

_____

_____

By way of a curious zig-zag, Michigan's 14th Congressional
District connects the predominantly African-American cities
of Pontiac and Detroit.

Note: Thanks to a successful ballot measure in 2018,
Michigan now has an independent redistricting commission.

MICHIGAN

US Congressional District 14

Racial discrimination in elections in Texas is no mere historical artifact. To the contrary, Texas has been found in violation of the Voting Rights Act in every redistricting cycle from and after 1970.

–SUPREME COURT JUDGE RUTH BADER GINSBURG, OCTOBER 18, 2014

State legislators not only draw the lines for their state's congressional districts, they also draw the lines for their own state legislative districts.

If the US Congress or individual states want to prevent gerrymandering along political party lines, they'll have to write and pass laws that make partisan gerrymandering illegal.

"**Cracking**" means divvying up a specific group of voters among multiple districts, so that the group's vote is diluted in each.

Are you a student at North Carolina A&T, the country's largest historically black public university? Then you might have to reregister to vote if you change dorms, since North Carolina's 6th Congressional District suspiciously splits your school into two distinct districts.

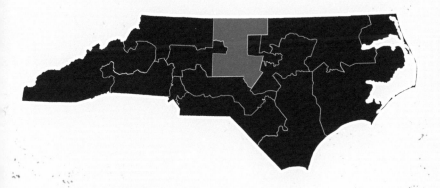

NORTH CAROLINA

US Congressional District 6

To me the biggest problem we have is in a gerrymandered
environment....We need to eliminate gerrymandering.
We've got to figure out a way to do it.

—OHIO GOVERNOR JOHN KASICH, DECEMBER 2015

"**Packing**" shoves a bunch of voters from a single group into one district; that group will win the district by a large margin, but there will be less of them to influence elections in other districts.

Most cities lean Democratic. Jacksonville, Florida, is a city. The big keyhole in the center of Florida's predominantly Republican 4th Congressional District is Jacksonville. Coincidence? Yes. Total coincidence.

JACKSONVILLE

FLORIDA

US Congressional District 4

The fact is gerrymandering has become a national scandal.
The Democratic-controlled state legislatures have so rigged the
electoral process that the will of the people cannot be heard.

-PRESIDENT RONALD REAGAN, OCTOBER 15, 1987

According to the *Washington Post*, Maryland's 3rd Congressional District is the single worst gerrymandered congressional district in America. Democrats in the state legislature went to unfathomable efforts to create this spiderlike monstrosity, which disenfranchises the state's Republican voters.

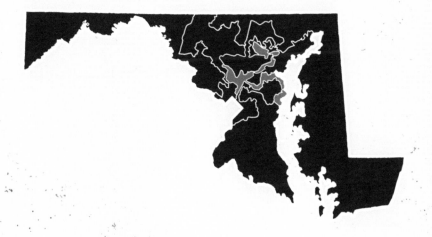

MARYLAND

US Congressional District 3

In 2019, two Supreme Court cases declined to make partisan gerrymandering illegal.*

As a result, until Congress bans it, we have to make gerrymandering illegal state by state.

Find out if your state has an independent redistricting committee, and, if not, how one can be established, at omgwtf.vote.

Rucho v. Common Cause & Lamone v. Benisek

ABOUT GERRYMANDER JEWELRY

Gerrymander Jewelry was launched in 2018, as a boutique line of necklaces and pins shaped like some of the worst gerrymandered U.S. House districts in America. It was created by the political PAC OMG WTF in partnership with political consultant Arielle Yuspeh.

Upon its launch, Gerrymander Jewelry was featured in several national newspapers and magazines. It was also worn by candidates for governor and secretary of state and used as a way to talk about gerrymandering with potential voters.

In 2019, Gerrymander Jewelry was named a Finalist by *Fast Company* for their annual list of World Changing Ideas.

You can order the jewelry through our website— www.gerrymanderjewelry.com—and follow us on Instagram @gerrymanderjewelry and Twitter @gerryjewelry for product updates and for news about gerrymandering in general.